Contents

The words in **bold** can be found in the glossary.

What are big cats?

Big cats are large cats that live in the **wild**. They are much bigger than pet cats!

Lions have a very loud roar!

In the grasslands

Lions, cheetahs and leopards live in **grasslands** around the world.

Can you find grassland areas on a map?

In the jungle

Tigers live in **jungles** and forests. Their colours make it easy for them to hide.

A tiger can creep up without beeing seen.

Fast cats

Big cats can run fast. Cheetahs are the fastest animals on dry land!

Finding food

All big cats eat meat. They **hunt** and chase other animals.

Female lions do more hunting than male lions.

Big cat Senses

All big cats have good hearing and eyesight, and can move quickly.

Jaguars have smooth fur and long whiskers.

Big cat babies

Cubs often learn to hunt in packs.

Big cats have babies called cubs. They feed their cubs milk until the cubs learn to hunt.

In danger

Today there are fewer big cats in the wild. People have killed them for their **fur**.

How can we help look after big cats like this snow leaopard?

Big cat and small cats

Pet cats come from the same animal group as big cats.

Pet cats can't roar. What sound do they make?

Glossary

Grassland - area of flat, dry land

Hunt - find and kill animals

Jungle - area of land full of plants

Prey - an animal that is hunted and eaten

Wild - living in its natural environment

Websites:

http://animals.nationalgeographic.com/animals/
http://www.pluspets.net/facts-big-cats/
http://www.sciencekids.co.nz/sciencefacts/animals.html

Quiz

1. What do you call baby big cats ?
2. What do big cats eat?
3. Which cat is the fastest animal on land?
4. Why do tigers have stripes?
5. What are big cats hunted for?
6. What do cubs feed on?

The answers are on page 24

Answers

1. Cubs
2. Meat from other animals
3. The cheetah
4. So they can hunt without being seen
5. Their fur
6. Milk

Index